PANAMA

The truth about the U.S. invasion

Cindy Jaquith
Don Rojas
Nils Castro
Fidel Castro

PATHFINDER
NEW YORK LONDON MONTREAL SYDNEY

ISBN 978-0-87348-582-1
Library of Congress Control Number 2011927393

Manufactured in the United States of America

First edition, January 1990
Thirteenth printing, 2026

COVER: Toni Gorton

COVER PHOTO: U.S. occupation forces carry out sweep of Panamanian neighborhood, arresting suspects. (*Photo: AP/Wide World*)

PATHFINDER
pathfinderpress.com
Email: pathfinder@pathfinderpress.com

CONTENTS

Introduction

ON DECEMBER 20, 1989, millions of working people throughout the Americas awoke to the news that United States military forces had invaded Panama during the night.

At 1:00 a.m., U.S. officials held a secret ceremony at Fort Clayton, one of the thirteen U.S. military bases in the canal zone. There Guillermo Endara was declared Panama's new president. Moments later, massive bombing of Panama City began. U.S. troops then mounted a savage assault on military bases and working-class neighborhoods. Washington's forces eventually reached 26,000, including the 12,000 troops stationed there prior to December 20.

Panama's working people were the chief victims of Washington's brutal assault. In the first days of the invasion, thousands of civilians were killed, wounded, and left homeless. Whole neighborhoods were bombed into rubble or burned to the ground. U.S. troops prevented many of the wounded from receiving emergency medical care, and the lack of even the most basic medical supplies and facilities led to many deaths. Panamanian victims were poured by the truckload into common graves. Over 5,000 people were rounded up and held in detention.

Resistance to the invasion was led by Panama's working people, organized in the Dignity Battalions. Though vilified by Washington and the big-business media as "thugs" and "looters," these battalions were in fact popular militias set up in 1988 to help prepare Panama's workers and farmers to defend their country against exactly what occurred: a U.S. invasion. Although most combat had ended by the second week of the invasion, the resistance led by the Dignity Battalions proved much stiffer than the Pentagon had bargained for.

Two weeks after the invasion, the U.S. occupation force seized Gen. Manuel Noriega, Panama's head of state, flew him to the United States against his will, and jailed him. Washington has announced its intention to put him on trial in Miami. This arrogant move is in gross violation of Panamanian sovereignty, as well as all norms of international law.

Washington used the invasion to escalate provocations against Cuba and Nicaragua as well. The embassies of these two countries in Panama City were surrounded by U.S. troops. At one point several Cuban diplomats were illegally detained. On December 29, U.S. forces raided and ransacked the residence of Nicaragua's ambassador.

In the days and weeks following the invasion, actions protesting Washington's assault took place in many U.S. cities, as well as throughout Latin America and in dozens of other countries around the world. In particular, many anti-imperialist fighters in the Caribbean spoke out against the violation of their sister country.

Washington's action was so flagrantly illegal that the overwhelming majority of world governments have felt compelled to state opposition to it. The Organization of American States, long a pliant tool of Washington's foreign policy, condemned the invasion with only a single dissenting vote—that of the U.S. delegate. The United Nations General Assembly went on record against the invasion by a wide margin.

Those governments that did back Washington themselves became targets of protest. The president of the Canadian Labour Congress, for example, protested the government of Canada's support for the invasion, terming it "a simple-minded endorsation of vigilante justice."

How did Bush justify this massive assault? The invasion, he claimed, was needed to safeguard U.S. citizens, restore democracy, and protect the Panama Canal treaties.

Not so.

The truth is that after several years of trying to overthrow Panama's government using everything from economic sanctions to coup attempts, Washington finally decided that only direct military intervention could accomplish what it wanted. Its aim was to install a client regime, smash the movement for national sovereignty and social justice that had developed in Panama over the previous twenty years, undermine the Panama Canal treaties, ensure the use of U.S. military bases in the country, and strengthen U.S. domination throughout the region.

The purpose of this pamphlet is to tell the truth about Panama's fight for sovereignty. It seeks to help arm working people, students, political activists, and other fighters with facts needed to answer Washington's lies.

The first article, "Why the Panamanian People Are Fighting for National Dignity" by Cindy Jaquith, was featured in a special issue of the New York socialist newsweekly, the *Militant,* published in response to the invasion. Jaquith is a leader of the Socialist Workers Party of the United States. She has visited Panama several times to report for the *Militant,* most recently in November 1989.

The second article, "Panama's Fight for Sovereignty: A History" by Don Rojas, explains how the U.S. rulers seized what is now the Panama canal zone, and the record of resistance by the Panamanian people up to the mid-1960s. The article appeared in two parts in August and September 1989 in the *Militant.* Rojas himself was a victim of Washington's last direct military intervention in the region—the 1983 invasion of Grenada. He served as press secretary to Maurice Bishop, murdered prime minister of Grenada's revolutionary government. Following the invasion, Rojas was arrested and deported by the occupation forces and has been barred from Grenada ever since. His articles appear frequently in the *Militant* and other newspapers in the United States and the Caribbean.

The third piece is a speech presented by Panamanian leader Nils Castro to the Third Assembly of the Anti-Imperialist Organizations of the Caribbean and Central America, held in Panama City in June 1988. Nils Castro represented Panama's Democratic Revolutionary Party at that conference. This speech is reprinted from *One People, One Destiny: The Caribbean and Central America Today* (New York: Pathfinder, 1988), edited by Don Rojas.

The final item in the pamphlet is a speech by Cuban President Fidel Castro given in Havana December 21, 1989, the day after the invasion. The speech, translated from the December 22, 1989, issue of *Granma,* also appeared in the special issue of the *Militant.*

Susan LaMont

JANUARY 4, 1990

Panamanians protest U.S. domination, 1959.

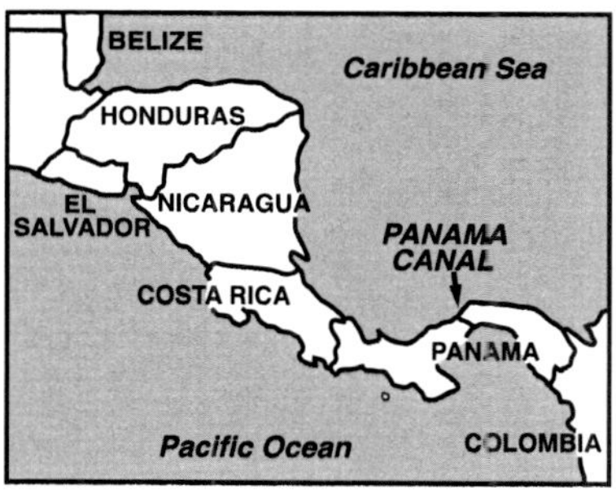

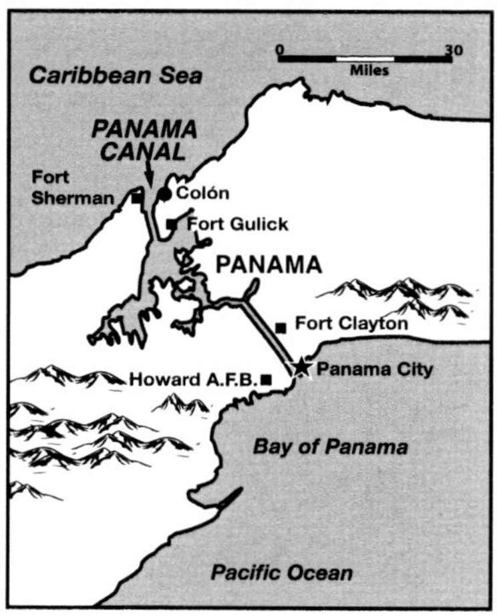

Why the Panamanian people are fighting for national dignity

CINDY JAQUITH

"General Thurman, with the way things are going, don't you think it's optimistic to say U.S. troops will be out of Panama in one month?"

TED KOPPEL
ABC Nightline

"Well, you'll recall when we went into Detroit. We said it would be for ten days and then it took us a while. . . ."

GEN. MAXWELL THURMAN
Head of U.S. Southern Command, Panama
December 22, 1989

THREE DAYS INTO THE U.S. invasion of Panama—Washington's biggest military operation since the Vietnam War—Gen. Maxwell Thurman could think only of Detroit, where 4,700 U.S. paratroopers and 8,000 National Guardsmen invaded in 1967 to crush a rebellion by Blacks against police brutality.

The U.S. Army's occupation of Detroit left 43 Blacks dead, 2,000 wounded, 5,000 arrested, and 5,000 homeless.

The invasion of Panama by 26,000 U.S. troops has taken

thousands of Panamanian lives and left thousands more homeless and wounded. Body bags of U.S. GIs have arrived in the United States, along with hundreds of wounded U.S. troops.

Washington says it has occupied this country of only 2.3 million people to "restore democracy." But the bombing of working-class neighborhoods in Panama City, the refusal to permit Red Cross workers to evacuate the wounded, and the rounding up of thousands of Panamanian youth reveal the real target of this operation.

The invading troops have met resistance from the Dignity Battalions. These are armed civilian units of Panamanian workers and peasants, many of them Black. The battalions have been branded "terrorists," "thugs," and "looters" by the likes of General Thurman. Cuban President Fidel Castro has praised them as "heroes of Our America who are fighting for the dignity, honor, and sovereignty of our peoples."

Who are the men and women of the Dignity Battalions and why are they standing up to the most powerful military force on earth?

The battle of the Panamanian people for freedom from U.S. tyranny stretches back to the beginning of this century. In 1903 the United States intervened in Panama to gain for itself rights to build the Panama Canal. A treaty was drawn up giving the U.S. government rights to the canal "in perpetuity," including the right to administer the over-500-square-mile Canal Zone, to run the Panama Canal Co., and to use U.S. soldiers to maintain "order" in other parts of Panama. Washington didn't even bother to ask the Panamanian government, which it had just installed, to sign the document.

Tens of thousands of workers from the Caribbean, most

of them Black and English-speaking, migrated to Panama to work on the canal. Thousands died from the slavelike working conditions or from disease. Of those who survived, many stayed in the Canal Zone working for the U.S. Army or private U.S. companies once the canal was completed.

The decades following completion of the canal were marked by repeated struggles of Panamanians against U.S. domination of their economy and government and for an end to the occupation of the Canal Zone. Intertwined with the fight for Panamanian sovereignty was the struggle against the racist policies of the U.S. government. In the Canal Zone, which was subject to U.S. law, Washington had set up the same kind of Jim Crow system that existed at that time in the U.S. South.

Whites shopped at "gold" commissaries and lived in "gold" neighborhoods, while Blacks went to "silver" commissaries, drank out of "silver" water fountains, and could only find housing in "silver" neighborhoods. One Black neighborhood was even called "Silver City." U.S. police were quick to stop any Panamanian who was Black from entering the zone's white neighborhoods.

The struggle against this discriminatory system was waged partly through the trade unions that grew up among canal workers. Many of the labor leaders who fought to end segregation were expelled from the zone.

The "gold-silver" system, while not in force in Panama proper, nevertheless set the tone for racist policies throughout the country. Blacks, whether they spoke Spanish or English, suffered discrimination in jobs, schools, and housing.

The legal segregationist system in the zone began to fall apart, however, in the 1950s. With the first victories in the

U.S. civil rights movement against "separate but equal" facilities, certain U.S. policies in the Canal Zone were no longer constitutional.

In 1959 the people of Cuba overthrew the Fulgencio Batista dictatorship, ending decades of U.S. domination. Working people throughout Latin America were inspired by the new Cuban government's resolute action to distribute land to poor peasants, nationalize U.S.-owned companies, drive out the gambling and prostitution houses, and defend the revolution arms in hand.

Labor and youth struggles in Panama, as in many other Latin American countries, began to intensify following the Cuban victory. Sugar and banana workers in Panama spearheaded a battle for a minimum wage in the early 1960s. There were urban protests against high rents. Panamanian students organized demonstrations against the U.S. occupation of the zone.

In 1964, U.S. students and parents refused to allow Panama's flag to be raised next to the U.S. one at Balboa High School in the zone. When a group of Panamanian students attempted to do so, they were attacked and the Panamanian flag was desecrated. Zone police and U.S. troops then opened fire on the crowd, setting off rebellions in the zone, Panama City, and Colón.

More than 20 Panamanians were shot dead and over 400 wounded. The bulk of the protesters were slain in Chorrillo, one of the poorest working-class neighborhoods in Panama City.

Twenty-five years later, when the U.S. military invaded on December 20, 1989, Chorrillo was the first neighborhood to be destroyed as U.S. bombers pounded the Defense Forces headquarters located in the heart of Chorrillo.

While most strongly rooted in the working class, the demand for the United States to get out of Panama had also won support among middle-class layers and from a section of Panamanian capitalists who resented the special privileges granted to U.S. businesses in the Canal Zone.

In 1967 Washington offered the Panamanian government a new canal treaty aimed at maintaining the U.S. presence with some cosmetic changes. Opposition to the treaty was so great that Panama's National Assembly was unable to ratify it.

The political crisis deepened with the 1968 presidential elections. Arnulfo Arias declared himself the winner, but eleven days after taking office, he was overthrown by a group of young officers in the country's National Guard led by Omar Torrijos, then a colonel.

The National Guard, made up overwhelmingly of peasant and working-class youth, many of them Black, had been affected by the anti-imperialist upsurge sweeping Latin America, as had some of its officers. The young troops had no desire to continue allowing their country to be a base for U.S. military operations in the region.

Torrijos came increasingly into conflict with Washington, particularly as he pressed for control of the canal and an end to Panama's colonial status.

"We will never be an associated state, a colony, or a protectorate," Torrijos told the United Nations Security Council in 1973. "Nor will we add another star to the flag of the United States."

In 1974 Torrijos recognized the government of Cuba, breaking with Washington's long-standing policy barring relations with the revolutionary government of Fidel Castro. "Every minute of isolation suffered by the brother people of Cuba constitutes sixty minutes of hemispheric shame," Torrijos said.

Big changes came to Panama's countryside under the Torrijos regime, to the distress of the landowning families who had exploited the rural work force for decades without government interference.

The new government launched agro-industrial projects aimed at overcoming Panama's dependence on U.S. consumer goods. Torrijos also set up peasant cooperatives to increase production.

About 5 percent of the nation's cultivable land was distributed to poor peasants. Torrijos opposed extensive nationalization of capitalist farms, however, arguing that a mixture of private, state-owned, and cooperative enterprises was the road to Panama's development.

The government instituted social projects that benefited above all the impoverished rural population. From 1968 to 1986, for example, the number of public schools increased from 1,851 to 3,187. The infant mortality rate dropped from 40 to 19.4 per 1,000 live births, a lower rate than in Harlem today. Roads were built and electricity brought to remote parts of the countryside. Social security was extended to more than a million Panamanians who had never received it before.

Panama's labor movement began demanding a new labor code that would permit greater organization of the working class. Under the 1947 code, bosses had thirty different ways to legally fire a worker. The employers used this to crush organizing drives. Between 1947 and 1972 only twenty-nine new labor contracts were signed.

In 1972 the labor movement won a new code that permitted workers to join the union after just two weeks on the job. Unions were organized at many more work sites and nearly 200 contracts were signed the first year. Among those organized for the first time were the many public employees in the country.

The advances won by working people during these years opened the door to greater participation in society and the government by Panamanians who were Black. For the first time Panama's Indian communities entered politics, bringing to national attention their demands for protection of their indigenous culture, languages, and territory.

In 1977 U.S. President James Carter was forced to sign historic treaties promising to relinquish Washington's control of the Panama Canal to Panama by the year 2000. The Torrijos-Carter treaties stipulated that total control of the canal and the administration of the zone would revert to Panama. The U.S. military bases—which numbered fourteen at the time—would be dismantled. Between 1977 and 2000, control would be turned over step-by-step to the Panamanian government.

On October 1, 1979, a quarter of a million Panamanians demonstrated to celebrate the formal turning over of the Canal Zone to Panama. U.S. Vice President Walter Mondale, who addressed the ceremony, was greeted by banners demanding "Yankees out of Panama!" and "Sovereignty or death!"

The victory for Panamanian self-determination was the product not only of decades of battle by the Panamanian people, but big struggles taking place around the world that had weakened Washington's grip on the lives and destinies of working people.

In 1979 alone, the Iranian masses had overthrown the shah's monarchy; the murderous Pol Pot regime was ousted in Cambodia; the people of the Caribbean island of Grenada had established a popular revolutionary government; and in Nicaragua, the workers and peasants had toppled the Anastasio Somoza dictatorship, one of Washington's strongest allies in the region. The Torrijos government had given considerable material aid to the Sandinista guerrilla forces, who led the revolution to bring down Somoza and place the toilers in power.

In 1981 Torrijos died in a mysterious airplane crash. Gen. Manuel Noriega assumed control of the National Guard in 1983, changing its name to the Defense Forces.

By this time Washington's contra war against Nicaragua was under way. The U.S. Southern Command, based in the canal zone, directed the mercenaries. To Washington's irritation, the Panamanian government called for a political settlement to the war and opposed the deepening U.S. military intervention.

By 1985 the Sandinista army had begun to drive the contras back. The mercenaries were finished unless Washington could breathe new life into the war.

Then National Security Adviser John Poindexter paid a visit to Noriega in 1985. He demanded that Panama's Defense Forces directly aid the contras in Nicaragua. Noriega refused.

Suddenly a campaign began in Congress denouncing Noriega as a double agent—said to be working for the CIA and the Cuban government at the same time. Charges of drug trafficking were leveled at Noriega a few months later.

Inside Panama, Washington turned to the very forces overthrown by Torrijos in 1968, popularly known as the *rabiblancos* (white asses) because of their light skins, wealth, and ties to the U.S. government. These businessmen and landowners established a "Civic Crusade" in 1987 to demand that Noriega leave power. They sought to organize demonstrations and strikes to rally working people to their side.

The Panamanian labor movement had little sympathy for the *rabiblancos*, despite sharp clashes that had occurred a year earlier between the Panamanian government and the unions.

In 1985 and 1986, President Nicolás Ardito Barletta sought to impose austerity measures demanded by the International Monetary Fund. Barletta introduced new restrictions in the labor code, closed some of the state-owned enterprises set up by Torrijos, and tried to lay off 30,000 public employees. A series of general strikes protested the measures and Defense Forces troops were called out to break the strikes. The public employees union, however, was successful in blocking the layoffs of its members.

Whatever opinions workers had of the government and Defense Forces in 1987, virtually the entire labor movement opposed the Civic Crusade and what some jokingly called the "Mercedes Benz revolution," because the well-to-do Civic Crusaders arrived at demonstrations in the latest-model sedans.

Working people did respond, however, to a call by the Panamanian government in 1988 to set up civilian defense units, which became known as the Dignity Battalions. These militias were trained by the Defense Forces to prepare for a possible U.S. invasion.

Washington stepped up the pressure with stiff economic sanctions against Panama, aimed above all at making life miserable for its working people.

The U.S. government froze $56 million of Panamanian

funds in U.S. banks. Panama's quota for sugar exports to the United States was eliminated. All U.S. aid to the country was ended, including funds for medical programs such as antimalaria programs. U.S. companies were prohibited from paying taxes to Panama and also stopped paying social security for their Panamanian employees.

The sanctions had a devastating effect. By 1989 unemployment had nearly doubled, to 17.5 percent officially. Some 50,000 workers were laid off. Among the hardest hit were construction workers. Their union, which had 20,000 people working in 1987, had only 1,200 on the job by 1989.

By late 1989 the percentage of the population living under the official poverty line had jumped to 44 percent, up from 33 percent in 1987.

It was in this context that presidential elections took place in May 1989. Washington openly gave $10 million to the Democratic Alliance for Civil Opposition ticket (the old Civic Crusade), headed by presidential candidate Guillermo Endara.

Opposing Endara was the Coalition for National Liberation ticket, which united parties that favored implementation of the canal treaties and rejected Washington's arrogant demand that Noriega resign.

The race itself was close, but before all the votes could be counted the results were annulled by the Panamanian government because of the provocative U.S. interference. U.S. President George Bush responded by sending 2,000 more U.S. troops to Panama.

In the fall of 1989 Washington made its last attempt to use Panamanians to overturn the legitimate government of Panama. On October 3, U.S. troops provided backup for a coup attempt against Noriega by a group of officers in the Defense Forces. The coup was smashed within hours.

Two and a half months later, the biggest U.S. invading force since Vietnam attacked a country whose working people have fought long and hard for national dignity and self-determination.

Panama's fight for sovereignty: A history

DON ROJAS

I

Panama is not just a canal. Neither did its history begin with the construction of the waterway.

Panama is a country with a rich and complex history and with vibrant cultural traditions. A history of pain and suffering under Spanish colonial oppression, Colombian neglect and indifference, and misrule by a series of corrupt oligarchies in alliance with U.S. imperialism.

It has also been a history of bitter struggles for national independence, sovereignty, and self-determination—from its many attempts to secede from Colombia up to its present resistance against Washington's economic domination and military aggression.

Visited by the explorer Christopher Columbus in 1502, the isthmus was the principal transshipment point for treasure and supplies to and from South and Central America during the era of Spanish colonial rule in the sixteenth, seventeenth, and eighteenth centuries. During those years of wanton plunder, Panama was constantly attacked by pirates, corsairs, and buccaneers.

In the colonizers' lust for gold, mistakenly thought to exist in abundance in Panama, they slaughtered hundreds of thousands of indigenous Indians in the belief that the natives were hiding the precious metal from them.

After having virtually eliminated the Indians, the Spaniards brought in tens of thousands of African slaves to work the land between 1518 and 1820. Both the Indians and Africans mounted several revolts against the Spaniards. As a result, many Africans escaped bondage and fled to the mountains, where they set up their own kingdom and lived relatively isolated until the early 1900s.

In 1821 when Central Americans revolted against Spanish rule, Panama joined Colombia, which had already declared its independence. For the next eighty-two years the country struggled unsuccessfully to end its status as a "department" of Colombia.

Anticolonial forces in Panama had been inspired by the leadership of Simón Bolívar, Latin America's most prominent fighter against colonial rule. In 1826 Bolívar convened the Congress of Panama to lay plans for a united federation of free Latin American states.

Throughout the nineteenth century, Colombia treated Panama as a poor and unimportant fiefdom, exploited by military officials and tax collectors sent to govern this "backward department." During this period Panama received neither the autonomy and self-government that it had sought nor the protection from foreign powers that it had been guaranteed when it voluntarily joined Colombia.

In 1841 the Panamanians declared themselves an independent "State of the Isthmus," and in 1855 they set up the "Federal State of Panama," but neither effort was sustainable, and the country fell back into its "department" status.

The southernmost of the Central American countries, Panama is roughly the size of the U.S. state of South Carolina. It is marked with volcanic mountains in the west and rain forests in the fertile eastern region. Most of this land, however, is uninhabited, with the population of 2.5 million concentrated close to the canal. The canal bisects the isthmus connecting North and South America at its narrowest and lowest point, allowing passage between the Caribbean and the Pacific Ocean.

Panama's singular geography, more than any other factor, has fashioned the country's political history in the twentieth century.

The predominant cultural influence has been Spanish. But the country's indigenous peoples, as well as the descendants of African slaves and Caribbean peoples who migrated from the islands at the beginning of this century, have together helped shape Panama's identity and its national character.

Panamanian historian Ricuarte Soler argues that a Panamanian national consciousness and a sense of being "predestined to control the crossroads of the world" was well established before the formation of the Panamanian republic in 1903.

In the second half of the nineteenth century, French capitalists, who had built the Suez Canal in Egypt, became interested in building a waterway across the Central American isthmus. In 1878 they obtained a concession from Colombia to build a canal under the direction of Ferdinand de Lesseps, the engineer who built the Suez Canal.

After nine years in which thousands of workers died from disease, the French Canal Co.—by then bankrupt, scandal-ridden, and technologically depleted—abandoned the project.

The French effort did not go unnoticed by the U.S. capitalist rulers. President Rutherford Hayes in 1880 and later President Theodore Roosevelt both stated that Washington wanted to build a canal under U.S. control. They argued that it was necessary for "strategic defense" and for expansion beyond U.S. continental borders.

As a result of the brief war with Spain in 1898, the U.S. government won absolute control of Puerto Rico and the Philippines and established a "protectorate" over Cuba.

Washington was now an imperialist power with colonies in two oceans, and so both desired and needed a canal to shorten the travel time to its colonies, as well as to facilitate trade between the East and West coasts of the United States itself. Control of the canal would also place the rising imperialist power in a competitive position in world trade and commerce and bolster its military position.

The U.S. Congress had long been considering a route through Nicaragua, utilizing that country's huge lake on its western side. But in comparison to Panama, it was claimed that the Nicaraguan project would have been more costly. Moreover, the country was susceptible to earthquakes and volcanic eruptions.

By 1903, therefore, Panama had become the more practical and feasible route. By then the U.S. rulers were determined to have "their" canal one way or another. To them, flexing of imperialist muscle against Colombia seemed to be a perfectly logical and convenient way to achieve this goal.

No consideration was given to the views and sentiments of the proindependence forces in Panama, who were excluded from the negotiations of the Herrán-Hay Treaty of 1903. This agreement granted the United States "exclusive and absolute option" to build and then operate the canal for 100 years.

Under the draft treaty, the United States agreed to pay Colombia $10 million plus $250,000 annually, to begin nine years after the ratification of the treaty. Meanwhile, Washington, without consulting the Colombian government, agreed to pay the bankrupt French Canal Co., which was still subject to Colombian sovereignty, $40 million for its rights and assets. On March 17, 1903, the U.S. Senate ratified the Herrán-Hay Treaty and then waited for the Colombian congress to do the same.

The Colombian government had sought a percentage of the money Washington paid to the French company, but failed to wrest an additional penny. Five months later the U.S. rulers were stunned by an announcement that the Colombian congress had rejected the treaty approved by the U.S. government.

There had been heated debate in Bogotá, the Colombian capital, marked by what one historian described as "floods of antitreaty oratory that invoked national honor." The Colombian congress responded with no fewer than nine amendments to the treaty, all aimed at clarifying and preserving Colombia's sovereignty over the isthmus, its residents, and its two port cities of Colón on the Caribbean coast and Panama City on the Pacific.

Infuriated by Colombia's rejection, President Roosevelt railed against "those contemptible little creatures in Bogotá" who ought to understand "how much they are jeopardizing things and imperiling their own future."

Abandoning further negotiations with the Colombian government, the U.S. rulers then shifted tactics by promising the Panamanian independence forces diplomatic and military support to carry out a "revolt" against Colombia.

Using a crafty French engineer, Philippe Bunau-Varilla,

a former representative of the French Canal Co., as an intermediary with the forces favoring Panamanian independence, the Roosevelt administration promised that it would "guarantee" Panama's independence.

The independence forces were unable to prevent Secretary of State John Hay and Bunau-Varilla from drawing up a new treaty behind their backs and rushing it through the Senate for speedy ratification. So the infamous Panama Canal Treaty of 1903 was put together without the participation of a single Panamanian official.

In accordance with the "independence plan" worked out by Hay and Bunau-Varilla, the Panamanians would be given a flag, a declaration of independence, a constitution, and $100,000. On November 5, 1903, U.S. marines landed in Colón while the small Colombian garrison in Panama City retreated back to Colombia. Panama became independent the day after without a shot being fired. A U.S. army officer on hand was given the "honor" of raising the Panamanian flag over city hall. Panama was at once made and recognized by the United States.

On February 24, 1904, the U.S. Senate ratified the canal treaty, which allowed for interventions by the U.S. Army into Panamanian territory beyond the Canal Zone if required to maintain "order."

For canal rights, the U.S. government paid Panama $10 million.

The treaty also stated, "The Republic of Panama grants to the United States all the rights, power and authority within the zone . . . which the United States would possess and exercise if it were the sovereign of the territory within which said lands and waters are located to the entire exclusion of the exercise by the Republic of Panama of any such sovereign rights, power or authority."

By November Washington forced the Panamanian government to abolish its army and replace it with a weak, and at times weaponless, national police force.

Writing about the 1903 treaty, historian Wallace LaFeber noted the U.S. government's "breathtaking" powers to acquire any land or control any water "outside the Canal Zone but incident to canal uses." The zone itself is a ten-mile-wide strip across the isthmus.

Moreover, the U.S. officials controlled Panama's immigration and communications. They could intervene in Panama City and Colón, where most Panamanians lived, to enforce law and order, acquire buildings, and run sanitation.

Construction of the canal was begun in 1904 and completed in 1914. It was hailed as an engineering marvel of the twentieth century and a triumph of U.S. technology and know-how.

Tens of thousands of Black workers were brought over from the Caribbean islands to carry out the back-breaking work of building the canal. Of these, close to 5,000 died from disease, malnutrition, and sheer exhaustion.

II

The central feature of Panama's history from 1903, the time it won what some commentators in the region have described as "the most dependent independence" in the history of Latin America, is the quest of the popular masses for sovereignty over the Panama Canal and the Canal Zone.

In struggling to rid themselves of imperialist domination, the Panamanian working people have had to confront direct U.S. military intervention and occupation, a succession of neocolonial oligarchies, extreme economic dependency, severe social inequalities, and pervasive racism.

The U.S. colonial enclave set up as the Canal Zone controlled both the political and economic life of Panama. This domination was so extreme that in 1908, 1912, and 1918 local elections in Panama were directly supervised by the U.S. Army.

After World War I, the Panamanian economy slumped, and so did public expectations of the economic benefits of the canal.

At the same time, mass resentment began to build up against the excessive rights and privileges enjoyed by the U.S. government in the Canal Zone as guaranteed by the Hay–Bunau-Varilla Treaty of 1903.

In 1926 Panama's National Assembly, under pressure from the population, rejected an initiative by Washington called the Kellogg-Alfaro Treaty, which was designed to temper some excesses while reserving Washington's rights under the 1903 treaty.

In 1934 President Franklin Roosevelt, seeking to pacify the growing nationalist movement, visited Panama and called for a new treaty that would "eliminate as far as was possible all causes of friction and all reasons for legitimate complaint on the part of Panama without sacrificing those rights considered essential for [the U.S.] government."

One of the main causes of friction, which was not acted upon by Roosevelt, was the Canal Zone's role as a U.S. colonial enclave inside Panama.

Whenever a Panamanian travels across the country he or she must invariably cross the U.S.-controlled Canal Zone, which covers a total area of over 500 square miles.

The zone not only cuts through the middle of the Republic of Panama but the capital city abuts on the zone and the city of Colón is surrounded by it. In both cities, the principal commercial wharves are located within the zone. The U.S. government uses only 3 percent of the land in the zone for the canal; 68 percent is taken up by military bases and reservations.

Roosevelt's proposed treaty was approved by Panama's National Assembly in December 1936. However, it was not ratified by the U.S. Senate until 1939. Among Washington's concessions was a renunciation of its right of "eminent domain" in the cities of Panama and Colón and an increase in the annuity paid to the Panamanian government from $250,000 to $430,000.

In addition, the treaty gave to the Panamanian oligarchy "full opportunity" for local merchants to make sales to vessels arriving at terminal ports of the canal or transiting the canal, as well as the right to collect tolls from merchant ships in the port cities of Colón and Panama.

In return for these minor concessions, the United States government received the right of unimpeded transit across and along the Colón corridor, as well as the right to set up roads within it. The corridor had been established to provide Panamanian access to the city of Colón.

The economic depression that hit the capitalist economy worldwide in the 1930s left Panama even more dependent upon U.S. capitalism. Reduced investments by U.S. businessmen and bankers in the Canal Zone led to increased unemployment among Panamanian workers, lowering their purchasing power and spreading poverty. This, in turn, produced working-class upheavals that helped lead to the election of a populist capitalist politician, Arnulfo

Arias, to the presidency in 1940.

Arias drew up a nationalist constitution reflecting the sentiments of the Panamanian masses for sovereignty over the Canal Zone. But he was soon overthrown by the dominant forces among the local capitalists in collusion with Washington and the Panamanian National Police.

A serious social revolt was averted after Arias's overthrow, partly because Panama's capitalist economy was in an upswing from the increased use of the canal by the U.S. military during World War II and from the construction boom related to the new U.S. military bases.

Due to the 1936 renegotiation of the canal treaty, the zone market was opened to Panamanian capitalists during the war. The increase in traffic of U.S. warships through the canal strengthened the demand for locally provided goods and services, which gave an impetus to domestic agricultural and industrial production. Energy consumption rose by 62 percent in Panama City and 73 percent in Colón. Employment in the zone increased from 14,800 in 1939 to 40,000 in 1942. By 1945, participation of the Canal Zone in Panama's gross domestic product reached 21 percent.

From its control of the canal during the war years, U.S. big business also accrued significant benefits.

According to information presented to the U.S. Congress by the Canal Zone governor in 1947, "monetary saving to the United States arising from the use of the canal [during the war years] is estimated as $1,500 million in maritime costs alone without considering the lives and materials that were saved."

In the immediate postwar period a recession hit Panama as the Canal Zone demand for goods declined by 20 percent and that for services by 50 percent. Unemployment reached 11.4 percent of the total labor force and 22.3 percent of nonagricultural labor.

Income received from raw material exports lagged behind payment for manufactured imports.

As the recession deepened, vast slums spread around Colón and Panama City.

Soon after the war ended in 1945, the Panamanian National Assembly ordered the minister of foreign affairs to inform Washington that the U.S. military bases built during the war should be removed from Panamanian territory "no later than one year after the end of hostilities." Panamanian public opinion firmly supported this mandate, but the U.S. government refused to accept it.

Mobilizations of workers, farmers, students, and women exploded in the streets of Panama City and Colón, forcing Washington to back down and order the immediate withdrawal of 2,000 troops and military equipment in 1947. The U.S. military retained the wartime Río Hato air base.

Working-class protests against imperialist domination picked up momentum. Banana workers challenged the privileges and rights of the U.S.-based multinational corporation United Fruit, which operated as a huge foreign fiefdom in Panama with its own security forces.

Throughout the 1950s and 1960s agricultural workers struck repeatedly for higher wages and better working and living conditions, and students agitated for Panamanian control over the Canal Zone.

This growing anti-imperialist mass movement, coupled with the postwar economic recession and the resulting decline in living standards, spurred internal conflicts within the local ruling class. In the three years from 1949 to 1953 the country had four presidents.

The power of the traditional political and economic oligarchy waned as the National Guard emerged as a political force in its own right. Racial and class tensions among Panamanians increased. Discriminatory practices against Panamanians in both jobs and wages within the Canal Zone continued.

A quasi-nationalist regime led by José Antonio Remón, former commander of the National Guard, took control in 1953 under the popular slogan, "Neither millions nor handouts [from the United States]—we want justice."

Remón invited U.S. President Dwight Eisenhower to visit Panama, which he did in 1955, leading to the Remón-Eisenhower revision of the canal treaty. The U.S. government conceded to increase its annual payment for use of the canal and to grant the local ruling class the right to tax Panamanians who worked in the Canal Zone. But its prosovereignty rhetoric notwithstanding, the Remón government did not demand or win any gains under the new treaty in the direction of Panamanian control over the canal and the Canal Zone.

Panamanian capitalists were the only local beneficiaries from the 1955 treaty. Local manufactured goods were exempted from application of the Buy American Act in the Canal Zone, and U.S. business agreed to stop manufacturing inside the zone as soon as it could be shown that similar goods could be produced in Panama. Panama became marginally stronger in relation to the U.S. colonial enclave through the acquisition of these new resources. The economic weight of the Panamanian capitalists increased.

Local food production expanded while the importation of food, which in 1951 had been 20 percent of total imports, fell to 15 percent in 1955 and to 12 percent in 1960.

The penetration of capitalist relations into agricultural production intensified and wageworkers grew from 4.5 percent of agricultural labor in 1950 to 22.8 percent in 1961. Thousands of small farmers displaced from the land moved to the cities, where they faced large-scale unemployment, wretched housing, and inadequate public services.

In 1958 a movement to highlight the oppression of colonialism and neocolonialism was organized primarily by high school and university students with support from women's groups and some labor unions. The movement demanded a revision of all existing treaties between Panama and the United States.

In response, President Eisenhower agreed to allow the Panamanian flag to be flown alongside the U.S. flag in the Canal Zone's Shaler Triangle as a symbol of Panamanian sovereignty, and in 1962 President John Kennedy joined with President Roberto Chiari of Panama to designate public buildings that would fly either both flags or none.

The triumph of the Cuban revolution in 1959 under the leadership of Fidel Castro and the July 26 Movement inspired the nationalist and anti-imperialist forces throughout the Americas, including in Panama.

Emboldened by this historic victory, patriotic Panamanian students and working people stepped up their prosovereignty mobilizations and actions.

In January 1964 an incident took place in the Canal Zone that was to become a watershed in the Panamanian peoples' anti-imperialist struggles.

On January 9, U.S. students and their parents living in the zone hoisted the U.S. flag at Balboa High School, disobeying the orders of the zone governor, and refused to allow the Panamanian flag to be flown alongside it. When

Panamanian students entered the zone and secured permission to raise their flag, they were stopped by the U.S. students, and the Panamanian flag was desecrated.

This triggered a revolt that lasted for two days and nights. Panamanian protesters were fired upon by zone police and later by U.S. soldiers, resulting in 21 Panamanian deaths and 400 wounded, many of them critically.

News of the rebellion sent shock waves throughout the Americas. Panama broke off diplomatic relations with the U.S. government and appealed to the Organization of American States, which set up a commission of inquiry that later recommended the two countries draw up a new treaty.

Direct U.S. military interventions in the Caribbean region since 1898

The list below includes cases of direct intervention by U.S. military forces in the Caribbean and Central American region. It does not include acts such as the CIA-directed overthrow of the government of Guatemala in 1954; the U.S.-organized contra war against Nicaragua; the numerous campaigns of political and economic destabilization; or the large-scale military and financial assistance to right-wing regimes such as in El Salvador.

COSTA RICA 1917

CUBA 1898–1902, 1906–9, 1912, 1961

DOMINICAN REPUBLIC 1903, 1904, 1912–14, 1916–24, 1965

GRENADA 1983

GUATEMALA 1904, 1920

HAITI 1914, 1915–34

HONDURAS 1905, 1907, 1910, 1912, 1919, 1923, 1924, 1929

MEXICO 1914, 1916, 1918

NICARAGUA 1906–9, 1912–16, 1927–33

PANAMA 1903, 1908, 1912, 1918, 1919–20, 1925, 1989

PUERTO RICO 1898–PRESENT

More importantly, however, this event helped open a new chapter in the struggle for Panama's sovereignty. By 1977 the U.S. government had been forced to sign treaties committing itself to cede control over the canal and the Canal Zone to Panama.

As this brief account shows, Panamanians fighting today to implement those treaties are part of a long history of struggle for their country's sovereignty. This is what Washington is desperately fighting as it seeks to maintain its domination.

Panama's only sin is refusing to go down on its knees

NILS CASTRO

LOCATED AT THE southeasternmost end of Central America, Panama was one of the countries liberated by Simón Bolívar. Culturally and ethnically, it extends the Colombian-Venezuelan coast, and it is also a Caribbean nation. It is Caribbean because of its varied, historical ties to the Antilles.

The location and shape of Panama's territory makes its geographic position the main natural resource of the country—it is an isthmus that links the two continents of America and is at the very center of the hemisphere and the Caribbean. Thanks to this, shipping transit between the Atlantic and Pacific oceans, as well as other forms of international communication and trade, are possible.

If exploited rationally and peacefully, this asset could provide resources to finance the full development of the country's other productive capacities. But it hasn't been able to. For centuries, Panama's geographic advantage has been subject to the control of successive colonial and imperialist

---

This speech by Panamanian leader Nils Castro was presented to the Third Assembly of the Anti-Imperialist Organizations of the Caribbean and Central America, held June 20–22, 1988, in Panama City.

powers, hardly leaving even marginal benefits for Panama, and creating structural distortions in the country's economy.

The most irritating of these experiences has been and remains the hegemony of the United States, which has carried out numerous armed interventions since the beginning of the nineteenth century and which currently militarily occupies the central part of the country.

National struggles against U.S. excesses and to recover the territorial and moral integrity of Panama have been at the center of its history. We have fought to win complete independence and to exercise real sovereignty over the nation's main natural resource, as well as control over our country's development. We Panamanians have the right to determine this.

The 1977 canal treaties were a result of this history; of the tragic and heroic events of January 1964; and of the complex and prolonged negotiations led by Gen. Omar Torrijos during the 1970s, backed by mobilizations of the Panamanian people and international solidarity. Even though these treaties, which are now in effect, are far from satisfying all of Panama's just demands, they represent important progress toward achieving our national objectives.

In accordance with the treaties, civil administration of the canal became binational, with an increasing Panamanian share of control. The canal is to be turned over to Panama completely by the year 2000. Responsibility for its protection and defense is to rest increasingly with the Panamanian armed forces, while the U.S. military presence is to begin decreasing, so that the last foreign soldier leaves the country by the end of the century.

The treaties clearly establish that U.S. forces remain in Panama for the time being exclusively to provide protection and defense of the canal. And that this must always be carried out in coordination with the Panamanian armed forces. U.S. forces cannot be utilized for any other purpose.

Since the signing and ratification of the treaties, Panama has scrupulously carried them out and the United States has systematically violated them. The U.S. Congress unilaterally passed the so-called Murphy Law, or Law 96-70, which it uses to haggle over and deny Panama a large part of the benefits and rights that belong to us in the administration of and profits from the canal.[1]

In the military sphere, the United States has created and maintains two structures in Panama that violate the pact:

The 193d Brigade of its southern army tries to justify its presence on the basis of protection and defense of the canal. But its forces are much greater than what is required for this.

Even more serious is the Southern Command, which is an enormous complex dedicated to military control, espionage, and intervention against all the countries of Latin America and the Caribbean. Neither the existence nor the activities of the Southern Command are authorized by the treaties, or by Panama's laws or government. Both the Panamanian parliament and government have repeatedly demanded its removal, denouncing it before the world's principal international forums.

These two foreign military structures have nothing to do with protecting the canal. The canal's security is guaranteed by its neutrality, as well as its efficiency in the permanent service of the peaceful navigation and commerce of the nations of the world. It is also guaranteed by the good will of the Panamanian people, who make it possible for the canal to operate and who voluntarily refrain from interrupting its functioning.

Neither Panama nor the canal have enemies, or reasons to have them. The only thing that threatens the security of the waterway is the unwanted presence of the military forces and installations of a foreign power that is constantly involved in conflicts and rivalries in other parts of the world.

Both from a military and an economic point of view, it is absurd to station installations and large numbers of troops on the banks of the canal. This restricts its functioning and prevents the area from being used for more productive activities.

The canal has no nearby potential aggressors and would be vulnerable only if faced with a missile attack from outside the region. Anybody who wants to defend the canal against this hypothetical possibility does not need to do it from inside Panama. Inside our territory, the Panamanian forces are sufficient to protect and defend the installation of the waterway.

This is precisely why the Panamanian Defense Forces exist: to guarantee Panama's neutrality and the security not only of the canal but of all the country's resources. Our armed forces do this for the benefit of the international community and without threatening the sovereignty or security of third parties.

One reason for the existence of the Panamanian armed forces is to eliminate the legacy of colonialism and neocolonialism, and guarantee the integrity and self-determination of the country. This is in compliance with the clause in the treaties stating that for U.S. troops to withdraw, Panama must have sufficient armed forces to replace them.

It's for this reason also that the current administration in Washington has concentrated its attacks against the Panamanian military and against its *Torrijista* officers. In the ten years since the signing and ratification of the treaties, the strategic goals of the United States in the region have changed decisively. For them it's no longer merely a question of controlling the canal. They want to control the entire subcontinent. To do this, they must eliminate three obstacles once and for all.

First, change the terms of the canal treaties to broaden the authority of the U.S. military presence and to prolong it beyond this century.

Second, eliminate *Torrijismo* as the dominant political current and restore an oligarchic alternative government that will agree to and administer new canal accords.

Finally, under the guise of "professionalism," eliminate the nationalist, popular character of the young Panamanian armed forces. That is to say, break its civic commitments and turn it into the kind of repressive force necessary to impose the objectives I referred to, against the will of the nation.

Going against the grain of the real historical, ethnic, cultural, economic, and political characteristics of the country, U.S. administrations have insisted on subsuming Panama in their Central American strategy. Contrary to this picture, however, during the last decade Panama has played an important role in the Contadora initiative and previous initiatives—but not as part of the subregional conflicts.[2]

Nevertheless, with characteristic U.S. arrogance, in December 1985 Vice-Admiral John Poindexter—then head of the U.S. National Security Council—made the following demands:

The Panamanian government must break with the Contadora efforts. It must provide logistical and training facilities for the Nicaraguan contras. And it must assign special units of its armed forces to initiate acts of aggression against Nicaragua. When Gen. Manuel Antonio Noriega firmly refused, he was warned that he would have to face the consequences.

Economic reprisals against Panama were initiated the following January with the cancellation of assistance that had been agreed to through the U.S. Agency for International Development. The slander campaign against Noriega and other Panamanian leaders began in March, through Col. Oliver North's "leaking" to the press of "secret" National Security Council documents, as the U.S. press itself has revealed. The campaign has not let up since then, systematically pursuing its objective of isolating Panama.

This attack is directed not only against the Contadora Group (although the U.S. government put pressure simultaneously on other members of it, particularly Mexico). Significantly, during that same time, Gen. John Galvin, then head of the Southern Command and the current commander of NATO's troops, made Panama an offer. He proposed turning over civil administration of the canal to the country by 1990—ten years ahead of schedule—if Panama would allow U.S. military bases to remain in the country for fifteen more years, until the year 2015.

There's nothing naive about the U.S. conception of turning over the canal. On the one hand it recognizes that the waterway has been more efficient, secure, and profitable since Panamanians began sharing in its administration. On the other hand, the essence of the U.S. conception is something else: it proposes the "nationalization" of the canal, in which Panama would agree to privatize it—in other words, turn the canal over to multinational corporations dominated by U.S. capital. This would serve not only to dilute Panamanian demands, but also to discourage Latin American, Japanese, and European participation in the creation of new alternatives for the canal.

U.S. strategy to bring Panamanian nationalism to its knees has been able to combine various operations at the same time. It has carried out a campaign directed at the U.S. public and at Latin America and the world, aimed at discrediting General Noriega and other leaders. (It is necessary for them to prepare U.S. public opinion for a military intervention much more costly even than the invasion of Grenada.) It has accused them of a variety of crimes, such as drug trafficking, and has tried to make it appear as though a bloody dictatorship rules Panama.

Throughout this long campaign the United States has used to the utmost its undisputed control over the mass media in most parts of the world. It temporarily succeeded in its efforts to neutralize international solidarity with Panama and paralyze a Latin American response to the flagrant aggression committed against a Latin American country.

At the same time, in addition to the psychological damage it inflicted with this type of aggression, the U.S. government attempted to fashion a united front of right-wing political parties within Panama. When this failed to bring results, it organized a front headed by business and oligarchic sectors that succeeded in winning over numerous middle-class professional associations and civic organizations. This front had the support of the church hierarchy, most of the foreign banks, and the political parties I mentioned.

Through this the U.S. government aimed at—and temporarily succeeded in—destabilizing the political and economic life of the country. It initiated a process of social subversion that was supposed to lead within a short period of time to the setting up of a de facto government and the final breaking up of *Torrijismo* and the Defense Forces. The aim of the U.S. propaganda and disinformation campaign outside the country was to cover up the neocolonialist nature of this movement, making it appear as though the movement's aims were "democratic."

At the same time, intense pressure was put on members of the oligarchy—both those who were pro-U.S., as well as vacillating members of the government alliance. Officials of the armed forces who were less patriotic were also pressured. All of this was done to break their resistance psychologically and intimidate them into surrendering. This led to the betrayal of ex-Colonel Díaz and ex-President Eric Arturo Delvalle, neither of whom have any political significance of their own, as well as a group of officers.[3]

However, far from weakening the popular, patriotic movement, these moves helped purify and strengthen it. They opened the door to the establishment of a constitutional government with a patriotic character and a much broader social base.

On top of everything else, in its arrogance, ignorance, and desperation, the U.S. government carried out a brutal series of economic aggressions against Panama, along with military threats. It has severely damaged the Panamanian economy, particularly hurting the Panamanian people.

However, the imperialist plan did not foresee the resolute resistance of the Panamanian people. Nor that the imperialist actions themselves would become the best indictment of the true neocolonialist character of the internal subversion.

This has led to the breaking up of the social and political front of the pro-U.S. opposition, which has been stigmatized irrevocably for its role as pawns of U.S. errors. And the prolonged patriotic resistance has finally opened up the eyes of Latin American and world public opinion. This resistance is also increasingly becoming a political problem within the United States.

The temporary relative success achieved by the opposition has made possible a more self-critical examination of the political errors made by the Panamanian government over the last several years.

The government formed an electoral alliance with sectors of the oligarchy in 1984. It subsequently adopted a policy of concessions toward the International Monetary Fund. It allowed productive sectors of the economy to be decapitalized in the name of servicing the foreign debt and speculative finance capital, turning the country into a net exporter of capital. It allowed *Torrijismo's* basic forms of popular organization and participation to become weak. It maintained a government that was clearly unpopular, in the name of a supposed respect for formal democracy and to avoid incurring Washington's disfavor. These were errors that of necessity alienated important sectors of the middle class and demobilized popular support.

These are the errors that the people demanded be corrected when the technocratic, pro-IMF government of Ardito Barletta fell and that the ineffective, cowardly Delvalle government could not and would not correct. The patriotic government of Manuel Solís Palma is now undertaking the correction of these errors, under the most difficult circumstances, and is regaining popular support.

Panama has reiterated its decision to continue and

Panamanians demonstrate, 1989. The banner reads, "Los Santos [a province of Panama] says no to the gringo bases."

deepen the process of democratization. But it is not willing to denigrate democracy, reducing it to a mere succession of electoral matches in which the oligarchs take their turn in the government according to what pleases Washington. The cornerstone of real democracy is respect for popular, national sovereignty and the genuine exercise of national self-determination.

There is no democracy under conditions of foreign tutelage or interference, or by being forced to imitate foreign models. There is no democracy without effective democratization of the economic, social, and cultural structures of the country, with the people's participation.

There is no democracy if it's left to U.S. consuls to decide who can and cannot be president of Panama, or which Panamanian civilian or military officials can keep their positions and whether they can remain in the country. This is a matter of principle and is not negotiable.

In Panama we have witnessed and are witnessing what

will probably be the U.S. model of destabilization and control for the whole region in the coming years. Panama has been and continues to be an arena for experimentation with new forms of psychological warfare and neocolonial domination that are already being tested in other parts of Latin America and the Caribbean.

It's not only a moral imperative, where a small Latin American country whose only sin is refusing to go down on its knees is being subjected to the brutal and blatant aggression of a great power. It is also a political imperative, because the methods being used to force Panama into submission are obviously intended for more general use and are more than a simple precedent.

What is at stake is the sovereignty, self-determination, and dignity of all our nations and peoples. At stake is the right of the Latin American and Caribbean peoples to decide on their own forms of democracy, to determine their own future according to their own interests. Our fate—that of all of us—is either the right to popular, national liberation, or neocolonial slavery. That's why we say to certain governments that are too docile, too timid, too complacent: Do not ask for whom the bell tolls in Panama; it tolls for thee.

The resistance of Panama's people is of truly historic significance

FIDEL CASTRO

A FEW DAYS AGO, we projected holding this ceremony here today. In the past few hours, we thought about whether or not to suspend it, owing to the developments you know about. We had also planned a reception with the athletes, which had been promised some time ago. Obviously, however, that has been suspended until a more suitable time.

In any case, we wanted to go ahead with the ceremony, although I believe that our hearts are not exactly into talking about sports. Sports are deserving of every honor and glory. Victories in sports are one of the most legitimate products of the revolution.

This has been a year of great successes, of great satisfaction for our people, and of glory for Cuban sports. And these are a precursor of even greater glories in the future. But our intention is not to speak about sports.

It is more fitting to devote a few words to the heroes of

This speech was delivered December 21, 1989, the day after the U.S. invasion of Panama. It was given at a ceremony called to present awards to the most outstanding Cuban athletes of the year, held at the Sports City complex in Havana.

Our America who at this moment are fighting in Panama for the dignity, honor, and sovereignty of our peoples. It is more fitting to recall those who are dying at this moment. We should recall those who at this very moment are being massacred by bombs and imperialism's most sophisticated weapons of war.

We must think about the fact that they are fighting at this very moment. Thus, our event is occurring at one of the most painful, dramatic, and difficult times in the contemporary history of what Martí called Our America.[4]

To a greater or lesser extent, we have witnessed and received information about everything that began occurring yesterday, December 20, during the early morning hours.

It's not that these developments took us by surprise. It's not that we considered imperialism incapable of such a crime. It was possible to anticipate these acts.

Our country had denounced these acts in our press three or four months ago, and in particularly strong terms. We're now in December and these denunciations were made around August or September. We also energetically denounced them at the Nonaligned summit meeting.[5] We know the enemy and we know the enemy's moral character. Therefore, what they did could not surprise us.

But even though we anticipated these actions and denounced them, we could not but feel deeply indignant to the bottom of our hearts, deeply angry, deeply bitter. Because it is not possible to react to such a crime in any other manner.

Once again, we have been witness to how imperialism acts. We have seen or heard—in one way or another, through television footage or radio broadcasts—the pretexts and justifications used to carry out this savage and uncivilized action. We have listened to the spokespersons of imperialism, from the president of the United States to the secretary of state, as well as the secretary of defense and the Pentagon chiefs. We find loathsome and disgusting the way they try to justify the deeds, the lies, and the ridiculous pretexts used for it.

They say that the Panamanians murdered an unarmed soldier. Everybody knows how they go around there, how they go around in Panama drunk. Who doesn't know what U.S. soldiers do when they're drunk? Once they even climbed atop the statue of the hero of our national independence, José Martí, in Central Park.[6] There are photographs of it.

These soldiers, armed and in a state of intoxication, fired on a military installation and wounded some Panamanians. One of these soldiers died as a result of the provocation. What could the Panamanian soldiers there do, being attacked while at their post? What the imperialists are saying is that an "innocent" and "unarmed" U.S. soldier was murdered.

It seems that in the party they were having they brought along a North American woman. So what do the U.S. spokespersons say? That not only did the Panamanians murder a soldier, but there was also an attempt to sexually abuse a North American woman. These things have been said and repeated hundreds of times. The goal is to present as the most natural and justified thing in the world the act of committing genocide against the people of Panama.

These are the methods of imperialism and this is how it acts. We know it well, and not only through our own long experience. We also know the number of lies used in this whole sad episode of aggression against Panama. We have seen the videos, we have seen these things on television.

And we know the dozens and hundreds of times that U.S. troops have violated Panamanian sovereignty, humiliating and trampling on the people of Panama. This was occurring virtually every day, and now we have the scenes, we have the televised shots of these events, which our people can observe.

They showed no respect for Panama's streets or avenues. From their military bases in the canal zone they came with their helicopters, their tanks, their armored personnel carriers, and their mercenary troops. With the look of murderers that characterizes them, they would go into any part of the Panamanian capital or any other town, violating all international laws. And now they are saying that those who provoked it were the Panamanians. They are saying that the United States had to invade a small country in our hemisphere to defend the security of the United States.

I repeat once more: This is loathsome and disgusting. And these pretexts and lies have been spread throughout the world by way of their powerful mass media.

The fact is that they invaded Panama. How did they do it? They did it in the manner that the peoples were familiar with not so long ago, in 1939. They did it in the manner of the Nazis and the fascists, looking for similar pretexts to initiate their aggressions. They did it in the manner of the Nazis and the fascists, attacking by surprise, without any kind of warning.

This time they did it in the early morning hours, at 1:00 a.m., when it was assumed that the population was asleep, that the workers were asleep, and even that the soldiers were asleep. And this was not an attack against one position. It was a simultaneous attack on all the military units and important strategic points in Panama.

In this way they have brought death and destruction to this sister country of Latin America. In a few hours they have shed the blood of thousands of Panamanians, the majority of them civilians.

But they didn't attack fearlessly, that is, fearless of the death of imperialism's own mercenary soldiers. Quite the contrary. They killed as many persons as necessary to avoid their own losses. Wherever there was resistance they didn't send soldiers. They used planes and helicopters to drop bombs, and they "flattened" areas with artillery. Then they attacked. Whenever they encountered resistance, they would retreat again and "flatten" the area, using air power and artillery. This is the type of war they have waged in the capital of Panama, in the most densely populated communities. That is what has created thousands of civilian victims.

Imperialism's mercenary soldiers who are wounded receive immediate attention. They are picked up in modern ambulances, taken to hospital planes, and flown to the best hospitals in the United States. Meanwhile, they don't even permit ambulances to pick up wounded Panamanian combatants. And they don't even permit them to pick up the wounded civilian population Thus people are dying, and the streets of the capital of Panama are covered in blood.

There were some wounded Panamanians who the people themselves, in one way or another, were able to bring to the hospital. Owing to the number of victims, however, there was not adequate medical attention, despite the extraordinary efforts by Panamanian doctors. There wasn't enough plasma, medical supplies, hospital beds, equipment, or surgical instruments. And thus we have seen photographs and television footage of dozens of civilians—men, women, children, and old people—whose dead bodies filled the hospital corridors.

Cuba addressed itself to all the most authoritative international bodies. It called on the United Nations. It called on the Movement of Nonaligned Countries and all organizations that could participate in the struggle, in the effort to halt U.S. imperialism's act of barbarism. Cuba spoke with many friends throughout the world.

But in addition, it also addressed itself to the International Red Cross, to the highest authorities of that institution, explaining to them what was occurring in Panama with the victims of the invasion. We explained the need for an urgent mobilization to attend to the wounded Panamanians, who the empire's mercenary soldiers were preventing from even receiving assistance.

We have expressed our willingness to cooperate. We have expressed our willingness to send our plasma, our doctors, our equipment, our surgeons. We have done this many times over the years of the revolution, helping countries that suffered natural catastrophes such as hurricanes or earthquakes. We have done this even in cases where the governments were enemies of ours, as in Nicaragua under Somoza, or as in Honduras. We also did this with governments that we had no relations with, as happened on one occasion following a major earthquake in Peru. Now we are facing the reality that it is not possible to assist Panama's wounded, because U.S. troops are there and do not want Panama's wounded to receive assistance.

How much barbarity and abuse have we come to in this world? How much cruelty have we come to in this world? Thus, while the empire's wounded soldiers travel immediately to the best hospitals over there, Panamanians lie bleeding in the streets.

That's why I say that the events are sufficiently sad and sufficiently harsh as to make anyone angry and bitter. I'm no longer thinking just of the brutality, the illegality, and the unjustifiable action of the United States.

Alongside this, there is something else that has occurred that is truly historic, that is truly significant. This is the resistance of the people of Panama, the resistance of the units of the Defense Forces and the civilians organized in the Dignity Battalions and other units.

The empire believed the resistance would last minutes, perhaps hours. They thought that when they dropped paratroopers at night or attacked with planes and helicopters, not a single soldier or a single civilian combatant would remain at his post. That is the conception they have of Latin Americans. They still have not learned enough. That is their conception—or more accurately, that is their contempt for our peoples.

The truth is that they believed the battle would already be over by dawn. The president of the United States had a speech prepared for 7:00 a.m. to announce that everything had already been wrapped up. One could see discouragement, disgust, even panic on his face that morning. Tens of thousands of soldiers had been deployed in a surprise attack, along with hundreds of planes, helicopters, heavy artillery, and armored personnel carriers. But despite all this, they encountered everywhere the heroic resistance of the Defense Forces and of civilians opposing the aggression.

In this respect they were unable to imitate Hitler. They were unable to imitate the fascists and the Nazis of 1939 or 1940. Because in many countries the Nazis were able to at least capture important cities in a matter of hours, fighting against well-equipped armies. Yet in twenty-four hours the empire was not able to capture the capital city of Panama. This was despite the fact that they began the attack from military bases within Panama itself, and despite their fabulous superiority in men and, above all, in weaponry. And yet they were unable to overcome the resistance of a handful, of a few thousand combatants.

Don't imagine that Panama had a large military force. They possessed a few thousand men in their armed forces spread across the country, plus a few thousand civilians organized and trained in a relatively brief period of time. Don't imagine that large amounts of military equipment were in the hands of the Panamanians. Many of our municipalities in Cuba have more weapons and more firepower than the Panamanian people had as they confronted this aggression.

We ourselves have calculated our firepower in comparison with that of Panama. These calculations show that Cuba possesses 200 to 300 times greater firepower than Panama in terms of combat resources, quantity of arms, and the capability of our weaponry. Nevertheless, tens of thousands of Yankee troops, attacking by surprise in the early morning hours of December 20, were unable to capture Panama City. Even today they have had to take another twenty-four hours to try to overcome the resistance. And this is in a city cornered between the Pacific Ocean and the canal.

That is why we believe that the Panamanian people have written one of the most heroic chapters in the history of the hemisphere during the last forty-eight hours.

None of the empire's key objectives have been attained.

They did not succeed in capturing the head of the Defense Forces, which was one of the main stated aims for this savage and illegal action. Their aim was to capture him and bring him to the United States.

See how far we have come: they have put into practice a new imperial principle whereby their armed forces can land in any part of the world to arrest persons they say are wanted by their courts. They can go into any part of the world and arrest people who in their view may have violated their laws, or whom they classify as terrorists.

This is the first time they have put this principle into practice. They have invaded a country and killed thousands of people under the pretext of capturing a senior official of a sovereign state in Latin America, a country that is a prominent member of the Movement of Nonaligned Countries and the United Nations. But they are frustrated because they say they have not attained their objective.

They also claimed that they were going to bring democracy. And they were going to do this through no less than a repugnant, puppet government. They have imposed a mercenary government over a river of blood, a river of Panamanian blood, the blood of the Panamanian people. In addition, they said they were going to guarantee implementation of the canal treaties and other, similar pretexts.

Up to the present, what they have won for themselves is the repudiation of the world. They have not succeeded in smashing the resistance. They have not succeeded in crushing the resistance in a few hours, as they imagined they would. The great army of the great empire has been made to look ridiculous against a handful of Panamanian fighters attacked by surprise.

What are they now afraid of? What do they now fear? They fear that the resistance will be prolonged. Their tactic has been to attack the capital, appoint a puppet government, and, based on this, call on the other patriots to surrender. It's as if one day they attacked Havana and captured it, and then called on the people of Pinar del Río to surrender, the people of Villa Clara to surrender, the people of the eastern provinces to surrender, the combatants in the Sierra Maestra to surrender.

That is their hope, and that's the idea they are attempting to apply. They are making use of their technology to jam television broadcasts and to send messages over clandestine radio stations, applying the methods of psychological warfare. The goal is to paint a picture of a people no longer able to put up resistance. In this way they also aim to deceive the world.

Yesterday we witnessed how in the morning, six hours after the attack had begun, they were already telling the world that all resistance had ended.

For more than fifteen hours yesterday, the Panamanian national radio network—which was being relayed to other transmitters—broadcast news of what was occurring, summoning the people to the struggle. It did this until the invaders were able to silence it through direct attacks by helicopter gunships.

But Panamanians have also been listening to international radio. They have been listening to Cuban radio, to Radio Havana Cuba, Radio Rebelde, and other stations. These stations were in regular communication with Panama yesterday, informing the people of Cuba and the world of what was happening. Today these stations continue reporting, although the U.S. was attempting to intercept their broadcasts in Panama. They were trying to jam the broadcasts because they did not even want the Panamanian people to know what was going on through listening to Cuban radio.

What is it that they fear like the devil himself? What is the fear that all the spokespersons of the empire now express? The fear is that the resistance will continue. The fear is that the Defense Forces and the Dignity Battalions and all Panamanian patriots will continue the war in the country's interior. Because they know that it is possible, over a greater or lesser period of time, to control the capital with this overwhelming accumulation of force. But they are panic-stricken that the patriots will get organized in the country's interior, in the wooded and mountainous terrain, and continue the war of resistance. All the steps they are now taking are inspired by this panic.

Their hope is to prevent this from happening and to present the aggression to the world as being over. For this reason they are using all possible means today to confuse the Panamanians, telling them that all resistance has ended.

They are afraid of getting bogged down there. It is one thing to control a city, given the means at their disposal. It is quite another to try to eliminate resistance throughout the country if the Panamanians make use of the rich experience of irregular warfare.

This is something we have studied extensively. It is something we have educated our combatants in from one end of Cuba to the other, through what we call the concept of war of the entire people. We have studied the experience the revolutionary movement has accumulated in recent years, as well as our own experience. Because when all is said and done, we did not begin our struggle for liberation in the capital of the republic. We began in the mountains of the Sierra Maestra, until our guerrilla struggle extended itself across the entire country.

That's what the powerful imperialist gentlemen are

afraid of now, and that's what they are trying to avoid at all costs. They are afraid, and well they should be! Little by little they will be forced to learn what we are capable of, we whom they have scorned, we the peoples of Latin America!

They have had to be taught a number of lessons. They were taught something at the Bay of Pigs, a number of years ago.[7] They were taught something in Nicaragua, by the Sandinista fighters. And just recently they were taught something in a spectacular fashion by the heroic actions of the Salvadoran revolutionaries and patriots.

This was something truly extraordinary. For ten years the United States has constantly provided financial resources, training, and arms to the genocidal government of El Salvador. For ten years they have provided technical means, helicopters, planes, the most modern infantry weapons, communications equipment, everything. For ten years!

And yet the number of Salvadoran fighters has grown. They have proved they can penetrate the streets of the capital and remain there for weeks at a time, holding in check an army that is armed to the teeth, financed, and trained by the United States.

This was just five or six weeks ago. And now we have seen what has happened to them in Panama. They know that if the Panamanian patriots are able to take into account the experience of Nicaragua, of the FMLN [Farabundo Martí National Liberation Front] in El Salvador, then they are going to get bogged down in this small country—and for who knows how long.

The Yankee imperialists have in one way or another been rebuked by world public opinion. But in our opinion they have not yet received a sufficient response.

There is still a great deal of hypocrisy in the world. Europe, which boasts of its civilized character, has seen some governments applauding the aggression against Panama. Others have expressed their "understanding" for U.S. actions.

Of course, there are also governments in Europe that have forcefully condemned these acts. In terms of the European socialist countries—as far as we know right now—the Soviet Union has condemned the U.S. action and called for the withdrawal of U.S. troops from Panama. But in some European socialist countries we haven't heard so much as a word spoken concerning the aggression against Panama.

In Latin America the immense majority of countries and political leaders have in one way or another condemned these acts—some energetically, others more tepidly.

International institutions—above all the Movement of Nonaligned Countries—have forcefully condemned these acts. The United Nations Security Council has not said its final word on the matter; they are still discussing it. But as you know, the United States enjoys the sacrosanct right of veto, which it has utilized on countless occasions.

The United Nations secretary general has said he regrets the acts of violence. But in all sincerity I believe that this is a time not for regretting acts but rather for condemning them. In the past I have expressed the hope that peace can be attained. But this is not the time for expressing the hope that peace can be attained. Rather, it is the time to demand the withdrawal of the invading U.S. troops.

Of course it is not easy to carry out important functions in the United Nations, because those elected to posts there depend on the backing of the Security Council. And it is sufficient for a single member, among those who enjoy the irritating and antidemocratic privilege of the right to veto, to overturn the election of any leader of the United Nations.

The Organization of American States, although not the same rotten mess it was thirty years ago, is still far from being a model institution. This time the United States was not able to secure the complicity of the OAS.

This time the United States was not able to accomplish what it did in the case of Cuba, where it gained OAS support for its aggressive measures.

This time it was not able to accomplish what it did in the case of the Dominican Republic in 1965, where, after staging a cunning military strike, it managed to get the OAS to approve a resolution to also send in troops.

This time, despite many maneuvers in the OAS to get it to support U.S. plans for political aggression against Panama, it did not succeed. And when it came to sending in troops, the United States won no support in the OAS for its action, let alone agreement by OAS members to send in troops of their own.

What happened this time is that the OAS condemned both the aggressor and the victim. It condemned the aggression by the United States and it condemned the government under attack. This is a novel approach. But it is one that, despite everything, represents a step forward. In fact, we might say it is a considerable step forward.

Many governments around the world have condemned this crime, including a number of capitalist governments, a number of Western governments. They know it is an act of savagery, an act of barbarism, which strikes a blow against peace in Central America, against stability in Central America, where there are so many serious unresolved problems.

They know this action strikes a blow against stability in Latin America, where there are so many serious unresolved problems. They know it is a blow against stability in world politics, and that it is a humiliating slap in the face to the Soviet peace policy.

We have been sounding the alert for more than a year, since the meeting with the militia members of Havana held in the Plaza of the Revolution, and on numerous occasions since then. Just a few days ago, at the ceremony for the burial of the comrades who lost their lives in internationalist missions, we said what we thought about the imperialists' interpretation of peace and what we thought about the dangers of the present situation.[8]

We said what we thought about the evolution from a bipolar to a unipolar world, under U.S. hegemony. And we said what we thought about the stepped-up role by the United States as a policeman that does not stop at any hemisphere, that intervenes in Asia and Africa as well as in Latin America, and that takes upon itself the right to decide what government a country can and cannot have.

We said that the only guarantee and security that our people can have is that which we are capable of conquering with our heroism.

It is difficult to place much confidence in international law when we see such things. It is difficult to place much confidence in international institutions when we see these events and the other things we have seen. It is difficult to place much confidence in the United Nations when we see such things.

It is difficult to place much confidence in the Security Council, which ended up not even issuing a resolution, even a mediocre one, expressing a judgment on the events. Instead it discussed who represents Panama—the representative of the puppet placed in power there or the representative of the government under attack, which is recognized by dozens of countries around the world. This is what they have been discussing!

Even the OAS proved capable of declaring that the representative it would accept is the representative of the government of Panama, of the *Torrijista* government of Panama, of the anti-imperialist government of Panama. And this is something that has not yet been decided by the "brilliant" Security Council of the United Nations!

From this we have to draw lessons that even wise men should continually reflect upon. I am not a pessimist, because I believe in the peoples. And I believe particularly in the peoples of Latin America—peoples who have been so humiliated, plundered, exploited, and attacked. I believe in this mixture of Indians, Blacks, Spaniards, Europeans, and even Asians who make up our peoples! Or who make up the Cuban people in particular, and to a greater or lesser degree those of Latin America.

I believe in these peoples not as an article of faith but because I have seen them fight, I have seen them in battle. I admire the way in which Latin Americans today are prepared to fight. I am referring to the peoples, because there are governments that are still not sufficiently courageous to challenge the actions of the imperialist power. But any country, no matter how small, can fight.

The Grenadians fought. The Nicaraguans fought the genocidal army of Somoza, created by the United States. They fought the mercenary invasions, the war imposed by the United States, just as in the past Sandino fought the Yankees. The Salvadorans have fought with unequaled heroism. The Panamanian patriots have fought with equally extraordinary heroism. Without a single exception, the peoples are losing their fear of the imperialist soldiers!

I have not spoken of Cuba; there is no need to. We know very well what will happen if one day they dare to invade our homeland! I think they know this too—and if they don't, they should—because we have not wasted time. We have confronted this empire for thirty years, and the more aggressive it becomes the more we prepare ourselves to confront it with our own forces, which are sufficient to defend our homeland.

Our homeland will be defended not only with unequaled heroism but also with the best technical means that our science can provide, with the best military and political conceptions, with the best strategy, with the best tactics. And we didn't just start to work on this today, we didn't just start thirty years ago with this revolution. We began more than 120 years ago during our first war of independence.

One single municipality, even the smallest in our country, could wage a long war against the same number of troops the imperialists have employed in Panama. So we are prepared and we are trained. We have hundreds of thousands of trained military personnel; we have an experienced and seasoned party; and we have an exceptionally courageous and patriotic people.

Our people have always been patriotic, but never like today. They have always been revolutionary, but never like today. This stems from years of real-life experience in the revolution and in the international field. It stems from the constant observation of phenomena and of the evolution of the world.

Let the imperialists do what they will! They will never force Cuba to surrender and they cannot keep Latin America in submission indefinitely. Each time they will have to confront a people who are increasingly conscious, increas-

Cuban students marching to U.S. Interests Section in Havana to protest Panama invasion, December 21, 1989. ***(Photo: Miguel Pendás)***

ingly tired of suffering abuses, injustices, and plunder. Imperialism will increasingly fail to force the Third World into submission, no matter what political maneuvers or conspiracies it employs, and despite its successes against certain countries in the socialist camp.

Let them do what they will! I am convinced that these aspirations to be the policeman of the world, to be owners of the world, to be masters of the world, will be unsuccessful no matter what weapons they employ, including nuclear ones. We have already learned that this is nothing to be afraid of. We know this because they once threatened us with those weapons, and I don't think a single person in this country lost any sleep over it.[9]

It doesn't matter what they have! It doesn't matter how sophisticated their weapons may be, because what a man carries inside himself, in his breast, in his consciousness, in his mind, is worth far more than any advantages offered by their sophisticated weapons.

We know this from our own history and from more than one experience. In fact we began our war of liberation virtually without weapons. And with the enemies' weapons—which had been provided by the United States—we carried out and won the war. The situation today is different. Today, we have millions of weapons—millions!—and we even produce our own. But in addition we can also count on the weapons of the invaders, because we know how they can be taken and used against them. [*Applause*]

I think that the best guarantee is a correct understanding of the power of our peoples, of the courage of our men and women, of the courage of our nations.

More than in hackneyed phrases of international law, more than in discredited international institutions, we believe in the peoples and in their courage. We believe in the ability of man to continue marching on the path of progress, on the path of independence, on the path of genuine freedom and dignity!

I am speaking here to athletes, but we know that our athletes are also soldiers of our homeland. For they are ready, as has been said many times, to defend their country not only in the field of sports but also in the field of battle.

We know the patriotism with which our athletes fight. We know the moral values and honor with which our athletes fight. We know the love with which they defend our beautiful flag in any corner of the world. We know the honesty and integrity of their conduct. There is no campaign of lies that can force them to deviate from this. Not even all the gold in the world would be enough to buy them off. I speak to these athletes today and I express these sentiments, these thoughts, because this is not the time to speak of anything else.

You athletes know that the better trained you are, the better prepared you are, the more certain you are of victory. Inner courage, intelligence, and thought are important and decisive, but so too is training. That is why in recent years our party and our revolutionary government have devoted so much energy, so much time, and so many resources to preparing the people for a war of the entire people. Because if the difficult hour arrives, it's good to know how to shoot for the heart, how to shoot for the head, how to shoot with whatever weapon you have. And if the invaders come wearing bulletproof vests, we can make mines that will blow them 100 yards into the air. That's the only way they'll break the records set by Sotomayor![10]

We have arms of all calibers and penetrating power. And we will have the marksmanship to shoot where we have to shoot, even if they come equipped with armor heavier than that worn by the Spanish knights during their conquest of this hemisphere or in their wars of the medieval era.

Let us make use of this additional experience to deepen our understanding that we must be ever more prepared and ever more organized; so that the barbarians, the savages, the monstrous imperialists never again dare to commit a similar act of aggression against our homeland. They will have to pay a very high price if they dare try it!

I salute you, our athletes, for the honors and trophies you have won.

Let me finish today the way Sotomayor, the glory of our sporting world, did in his remarks today:

Socialism or death!

Patria o muerte! [Homeland or death]

Venceremos! [We will win]

[*Ovation*]

NOTES

1. In September 1979 the U.S. Congress passed Law 96-70, sponsored in the House of Representatives by Rep. John Murphy of New York. It "implemented" the Panama Canal treaties, but in fact contained a number of provisions that violated Panama's sovereignty over its territory.

2. In September 1984 the Contadora Group (Mexico, Venezuela, Panama, and Colombia) proposed a Central American peace accord designed to end the contra war in Nicaragua. The agreement was accepted by Nicaragua but rejected by Washington.

3. Roberto Díaz was relieved of his post as second in command of the Panama Defense Forces in June 1987; Delvalle was dismissed as president by Panama's National Assembly in February 1988. Both have joined the U.S. campaign of aggression against Panama.

4. José Martí is considered Cuba's national hero. He initiated Cuba's final war for independence from Spain in 1895 and was killed in battle that same year.

5. The Movement of Nonaligned Countries held its Ninth Summit Conference in September 1989. At that meeting Cuba's First Vice President Raúl Castro made a vigorous call for worldwide solidarity with Panama.

6. In 1949 some drunken U.S. sailors climbed on top of Martí's statue in Havana and urinated on it. This act of desecration provoked a wide public outcry and protest demonstrations among Cuban patriots.

7. In April 1961, in an action organized and directed by the U.S. government, some 1,500 Cuban-born mercenaries invaded Cuba at the Bay of Pigs. The invaders were defeated within seventy-two hours.

8. On December 7, 1989, Castro spoke at a ceremony honoring Cubans killed on internationalist missions. The speech was published in English in the December 17, 1989, issue of *Granma Weekly Review* and in the January 5, 1990, issue of the *Militant*.

9. This refers to the October 1962 Cuban missile crisis. At that time, Washington threatened a nuclear attack and invasion against Cuba after it had acquired missiles from the Soviet Union to defend itself from threatened U.S. aggression.

10. Cuban athlete Javier Sotomayor is holder of the world high jump record.

INDEX

REVOLUTION IN CENTRAL AMERICA AND THE CARIBBEAN

Puerto Rico: Independence Is a Necessity

RAFAEL CANCEL MIRANDA

One of the five Puerto Rican Nationalists imprisoned by Washington for more than 25 years and released in 1979 speaks out on the brutal reality of US colonial domination, the example of Cuba's socialist revolution, and the ongoing struggle for independence. $5. Also in Spanish and Farsi.

Maurice Bishop Speaks

The Grenada Revolution and Its Overthrow, 1979–83

The triumph of the 1979 revolution in the Caribbean island of Grenada under the leadership of Maurice Bishop gave hope to millions throughout the Americas. Invaluable lessons from the workers and farmers government destroyed by a Stalinist-led counterrevolution in 1983. $20

Cuba's Internationalist Foreign Policy

Speeches, vol. 1, 1975–80

FIDEL CASTRO

Cuba's foreign policy, says Castro, starts "with the subordination of Cuban positions to the international needs of the struggle for socialism and national liberation." Speeches from 1975–80 on solidarity with Angola, Vietnam, the Nicaragua and Grenada revolutions, and more. $23

CUBA'S SOCIALIST REVOLUTION

New!

Revolution and the Road to Peace in Colombia

The Example of the Cuban Revolution

FIDEL CASTRO

"No crime can be committed in the name of revolution," Fidel Castro declares, drawing from the example set by working people of Cuba as they took state power out of the hands of its capitalist rulers. In 2008, as part of efforts to end six decades of armed conflict in Colombia, he shared the exemplary record of Cuba's revolutionary struggle with the Revolutionary Armed Forces of Colombia (FARC) and the world. $10. Also in Spanish and French.

The First and Second Declarations of Havana

Nowhere are the questions of revolutionary strategy that today confront men and women on the front lines of struggles in the Americas addressed with greater truthfulness and clarity than in these uncompromising indictments of imperialist plunder and "the exploitation of man by man." Adopted by million-strong assemblies of the Cuban people in 1960 and 1962. $10. Also in Spanish, French, Farsi, Arabic, Greek.

Playa Girón/Bay of Pigs

Washington's First Military Defeat in the Americas

FIDEL CASTRO, JOSÉ RAMÓN FERNÁNDEZ

In less than 72 hours of combat in April 1961, Cuba's revolutionary armed forces defeated a US-organized invasion by 1,500 mercenaries. The Cuban people set an example for workers, farmers, and youth the world over that with political consciousness, class solidarity, courage, and revolutionary leadership, we can stand up to seemingly insurmountable odds—*and win*. $17. Also in Spanish.

New!
Cuba and the Independence War in Guinea-Bissau and Cape Verde

The Fall of the Last Colonial Empire in Africa

VÍCTOR DREKE

In 1974–75 the people of two West African countries, Guinea-Bissau and Cape Verde, put an end to 500 years of Portuguese colonial exploitation. Led by a popular movement forged by Amílcar Cabral, their struggle triggered the collapse of Portugal's entire colonial empire and brought down the 40-year fascist dictatorship in Portugal itself. Víctor Dreke's firsthand account brings to life this decisive victory. $12. Also in Spanish.

Women in Cuba: The Making of a Revolution Within the Revolution

VILMA ESPÍN, ASELA DE LOS SANTOS
YOLANDA FERRER

The integration of women in the ranks and leadership of the Cuban Revolution was intertwined with the proletarian course led by Fidel Castro from the start. This is the story of that revolution and how it transformed the women and men who made it. $17. Also in Spanish, Farsi, Greek.

Cuba and the Coming American Revolution

JACK BARNES

This is a book about the example set by the Cuban people that socialist revolution is not only necessary—it can be made. A book about the struggles of workers and other exploited producers in the imperialist heartland, and the youth attracted to them. About the class struggle in the US, where the revolutionary capacities of working people are as utterly discounted by the ruling powers as were those of the Cuban toilers. $10. Also in Spanish, French, Farsi.

CAPITALIST CRISIS AND THE FIGHT FOR WORKERS POWER

The Low Point of Labor Resistance Is Behind Us

The Socialist Workers Party Looks Forward

JACK BARNES
MARY-ALICE WATERS
STEVE CLARK

The global order imposed by Washington is shattering. A long retreat by the working class and unions has come to an end. The bosses and their government are stepping up attacks on our wages, conditions, and constitutional rights. This book highlights opportunities for building a mass proletarian party able to lead the struggle to end capitalist rule, opening a socialist future for humanity. $10. Also in Spanish, French, Greek.

Is Socialist Revolution in the US Possible?

A Necessary Debate Among Working People

MARY-ALICE WATERS

Fighting for a society only working people can create, it is our own capacities we will discover. And we will answer the question posed here with a resounding "Yes." Revolution is possible but not inevitable. That depends on us. $7. Also in Spanish, French, Farsi.

Are They Rich Because They're Smart?

Class, Privilege, and Learning Under Capitalism

JACK BARNES

Exposes growing class inequalities in the US and the self-serving rationalizations of well-paid professionals who think their "brilliance" equips them to "regulate" working people, who don't know what's in our own best interest. $10. Also in Spanish, French, Farsi, Arabic, Greek.

The Teamster Series

FARRELL DOBBS

Four books on the 1930s strikes, organizing drives, and political campaigns that transformed the Teamsters into a militant industrial union movement. Written by the organizer of these battles and leader of the Socialist Workers Party. A tool for workers seeking to use union power and advance the fight for a party of labor. $16 each, series $50. Also in Spanish. *Teamster Rebellion* is also available in French, Farsi, Greek.

Capitalism's World Disorder

Working-Class Politics at the Millennium

JACK BARNES

The social devastation and financial panic, coarsening of politics, cop brutality, and imperialist aggression—all are products not of something gone wrong with capitalism but of its lawful workings. Yet the future can be changed by the united struggle of workers and farmers increasingly conscious of their capacity to wage revolutionary struggles for state power and to transform the world. $20. Also in Spanish and French.

The Clintons' Anti-Working-Class Record

Why Washington Fears Working People

JACK BARNES

What working people need to know about the profit-driven course of Democrats and Republicans alike over the last three decades. And the political awakening of workers seeking to understand and resist the capitalist rulers' assaults. $10. Also in Spanish, French, Farsi, Greek.

BUILDING A REVOLUTIONARY WORKERS PARTY

The Turn to Industry

Forging a Proletarian Party

JACK BARNES

A book about the working-class program, composition, and course of the only kind of party in the imperialist epoch worthy of the name "revolutionary." A party that can recognize the most revolutionary fact of this epoch—the worth of working people, and our capacity to change society when we organize and act to win power from the capitalist class. $15. Also in Spanish, French, Farsi, Greek.

Malcolm X, Black Liberation, and the Road to Workers Power

JACK BARNES

"The conquest of state power by a class-conscious vanguard of the working class is the mightiest weapon possible in the fight against Black oppression, the subjugation of women, Jew-hatred, and every form of human degradation inherited from class society." $20. Also in Spanish, French, Farsi, Arabic, Greek.

In Defense of Marxism

Against the Petty-Bourgeois Opposition in the Socialist Workers Party

LEON TROTSKY

A reply to those in the revolutionary workers movement in the late 1930s who buckled to bourgeois patriotism during Washington's buildup to enter World War II. Trotsky explains why only a party fighting to bring workers into its ranks and leadership can steer a communist course. In the process, he defends the materialist and dialectical foundations of Marxism. $17. Also in Spanish, French, Farsi.

The Fight Against Jew-Hatred and Pogroms in the Imperialist Epoch

Stakes for the International Working Class

V.I. LENIN, LEON TROTSKY
FARRELL DOBBS, JAMES P. CANNON
JACK BARNES, DAVE PRINCE

Jew-hatred and pogroms—such as Hamas carried out on October 7, 2023—are part of the social convulsions and wars of the imperialist epoch. The authors explain why fighting Jew-hatred is decisive to the working class and oppressed nations of the world—and *what is to be done to end it*. $10. Also in Spanish, French, Greek.

The Struggle for a Proletarian Party

JAMES P. CANNON

"The workers of America have power enough to topple the structure of capitalism at home and to lift the whole world with them when they rise," Cannon asserts. On the eve of World War II, a founder of the communist movement in the US and a leader of the Communist International in Lenin's time defends the program and party-building norms of Bolshevism. $20. Also in Spanish and Farsi.

Imperialism's March Toward Fascism and War

JACK BARNES

"There will be new Hitlers, new Mussolinis. That is inevitable. What is not inevitable is that they will triumph. The working-class vanguard will organize our class to fight back against the devastating toll we are made to pay for the capitalist crisis. The future of humanity will be decided in the contest between these contending class forces." In *New International* no. 10. $14. Also in Spanish, French, Farsi, Greek.

FURTHER READING

Opening Guns of World War III: Washington's Assault on Iraq

JACK BARNES

The murderous assault on Iraq in 1990–91 heralded increasingly sharp conflicts among imperialist powers, growing instability of capitalism, and more wars. Also includes:

1945: When US Troops Said 'No!'
by Mary-Alice Waters
Lessons from the Iran-Iraq War
by Samad Sharif

In *New International* no. 7. $14. Also in Spanish, French, Farsi.

Labor, Nature, and the Evolution of Humanity

The Long View of History

FREDERICK ENGELS, KARL MARX, GEORGE NOVACK
MARY-ALICE WATERS

Without understanding that social labor, transforming nature, has driven humanity's evolution for millions of years, working people are unable to see beyond the capitalist epoch of class exploitation that warps all human relations, ideas, and values. Only the revolutionary conquest of state power by the working class can open the door to a world free of capitalist exploitation, degradation of nature, subjugation of women, racism, and war. A world built on human solidarity. A socialist world. $12. Also in Spanish and French.

Thomas Sankara Speaks

The Burkina Faso Revolution, 1983–87

Under Sankara's guidance, Burkina Faso's revolutionary government led peasants, workers, women, and youth to expand literacy; to sink wells, plant trees, erect housing; to combat women's oppression; to carry out land reform; to join others worldwide to free themselves from the imperialist yoke. $20. Also in French.

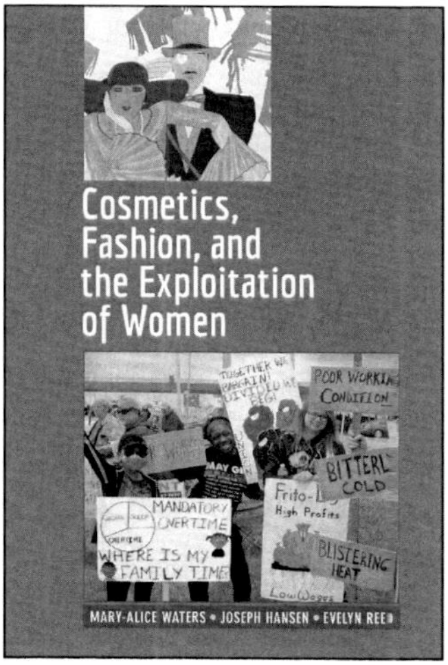

New Expanded Edition!

Cosmetics, Fashion, and the Exploitation of Women

MARY-ALICE WATERS
JOSEPH HANSEN, EVELYN REED

"Norms of beauty and fashion are inseparable from the class struggle." That's the title of the opening chapter of this new edition of a lively 1950s debate in the *Militant*, a socialist newsweekly. How cosmetics and fashion monopolies rake in profits from social insecurities of women and adolescents. Why women's integration into the workforce and unions is a major advance in the fight for emancipation. A Marxist classic on the origins of women's oppression and the working-class road forward. $15. Also in Spanish, French, Farsi, Greek.

Lenin's Final Fight

Speeches and Writings, 1922–23

V.I. LENIN

In 1922 and 1923, V.I. Lenin, central leader of the world's first socialist revolution, waged what was to be his last political battle—one that was lost after his death. At stake was whether that revolutionary government and the world communist movement it led would remain on the revolutionary proletarian course that brought workers and peasants to power in Russia in 1917. $17. Also in Spanish, Farsi, Greek.

Capitalism's Long Hot Winter Has Begun

JACK BARNES

Today's global capitalist crisis is but the opening stage of decades of economic, financial, and social convulsions and class battles. Class-conscious workers confront this historic turning point for imperialism with confidence, Jack Barnes writes, drawing satisfaction from being "in their face" as we chart a revolutionary course to take power. In *New International* no. 12. $14. Also in Spanish, French, Farsi, Arabic, Greek.